## Volume # 01

# iPhone 7

## *An Ultimate Walkthrough To The World's Latest iPhone Model*

## Volume # 02

# iOS 10

## *An Ultimate Guide to Apple's Latest iOS Version*

# CONTENTS

## Volume # 01

CHAPTER

## Volume # 02

# iPhone 7

## *An Ultimate Walkthrough To The World's Latest iPhone Model*

# INTRODUCTION

First and Foremost I want to thank you and congratulate you for downloading this iPhone 7 Guide Book

This book contains detailed instructions and strategies on how to get the best experience from your iPhone 7 and make the most out of it. iPhone 7, together with iPhone 7 Plus, was introduced on September 7, 2016. It was released on September 16, 2016. The overall design can be similar to iPhone 6s but iPhone 7 has new colors available and additional dust and water resistance. It also comes with earphones that connect using Lightning.

Thanks again for downloading this book, let's quickly get into it.

# 1

## GETTING STARTED WITH IPHONE 7

A fter purchasing a brand new iPhone 7 or any other iPhones, the very first thing that you have to do is to set it up so that you can already use it right away. The start-up process includes going through "Hello" then adding your accounts such as Apple ID, Gmail, Yahoo Mail and others. In order to use FaceTime and iMessage to connect with your family and friends, you have to sign in with your Apple ID.

If you are still in the exploration mode to get to know your iPhone 7, there is no need to worry anymore. We can guide you through the whole process with tips and tricks on how to get things done easily so you can have the best experience with your iPhone 7.

# Setting up iPhone 7

During the setup of your iPhone, you can start over anytime by simply pressing the Home button then tap Start Over.

## 1. Turn on your iPhone 7

When you buy a brand new iPhone 7 or any other iDevices, a simple "Hello" will greet you when you turn it on. It can also be in different languages. Press the **Home** button to start. For users with low vision, you can enable **VoiceOver** or **Zoom** right away. You can see your IMEI or MEID and ICCID by tapping the info icon "**i**" located in the lower right corner.

## 2. Select Your Country or Region

If you purchased your iPhone 7 in your country, it should already pick the right language. The country or region should also be right. Otherwise, choose your language then search for your country and region.

## 3. Choose a Wi-Fi Network and Enable Location Services

The next thing that will appear on your screen is **Choose a Wi-Fi Network** which allows you to connect to internet. If you already have an active service, you can select **Use Cellular Connection**. Otherwise, choose a Wi-Fi network.

After that, you get to decide whether you want to **Enable Location Services** or keep it disabled in the meantime. You can easily turn it on anytime when necessary.

## 4. Touch ID and Create a Passcode

Set up your **Touch ID** to allow your fingerprint to unlock your iPhone 7. For additional security, enter a six-digit passcode which you will need for features such as Apple Pay and Touch ID. You can tap **Passcode Options** if you prefer four-digit, no passcode or customized passcode.

## 5. Apps & Data

There are four options that will appear to continue your iPhone 7 set up.

- **Restore from iCloud Backup** – Tapping this allows you to retrieve your backup files in iCloud. Simply sign in with your Apple ID and enter your password for the purchases you made. Keep your device connected until the setup is finished. Your files saved in iCloud will automatically download to your iPhone 7 such as music, photos and apps.

- **Restore from iTunes Backup** – If you want to restore from iTunes backup, tap this option then connect your iPhone 7 to your computer via USB. Launch iTunes from your computer and select your device. Click Restore Backup and wait for the process to be completed.

- **Set up as new** – You can select this option if you did not own any iDevices before buying iPhone 7. This means that you will start using your iPhone 7 from scratch with its default settings.

- **Move Data from Android** – This option allows you to move your data and files from your Android devices.

# How to Restore from iCloud Backup

First, you need to back up your old device in iCloud so you can transfer the backup files to your brand new iPhone 7. To make a backup on your previous device, follow these steps:

1. Make sure that your previous device is connected to Wi-Fi.
2. Open Settings app, tap iCloud and select Backup. Check if iCloud Backup is enabled.
3. Tap Back Up Now.
4. Keep your device connected to internet until the process is completed.

After backing up your previous device, you can now continue to Restore from iCloud Backup option.

1. **Select Restore from iCloud Backup option.**
   Tap Restore from iCloud Backup from the Apps & Data screen then tap Next. Sign in to iCloud using your Apple ID and password.

## 2. Select Your Backup

Choose a backup and check if the date as well as the size is right. If you made purchases from App Store or iTunes with different Apple IDs, you will be required to log in to each. You can also skip if you do not remember the password by tapping "Don't have an Apple ID or forgot it."

## 3. Wait to Finish

Keep your iPhone 7 connected to Wi-Fi until the process is completed. Make sure that you also have enough battery life to prevent it from turning off.

This option allows you to transfer your music, photos, videos and apps saved in your iCloud.

# How to Restore from iTunes Backup

First, you need to make a backup of your previous device in iTunes so you can transfer your data to your iPhone 7. To make an iTunes backup, follow these steps:

1. Connect your old device to your PC or Mac.
2. Launch **iTunes**. Make sure that you are running the latest version of iTunes.
3. Click your device.
4. Click **Back Up Now**. Wait for the process to finish. To check if the backup was successful, go to Preferences then click Devices. You will find your device as well as the time and date the backup was created.

After making an iTunes backup of your previous device, you can now restore your iPhone 7 from iTunes backup.

1. **Select Restore from iTunes Backup.**

   From Apps & Data screen, select Restore from iTunes Backup then tap Next.

2. **Connect to iTunes**

   Connect your iPhone to your PC or Mac and launch iTunes. Select your device.

3. **Restore Backup**

   Click Restore Backup and choose a backup.

4. **Wait to Finish**

   Keep your device connected to your computer until the restore process is finished. As much as possible, keep your device connected to internet and charging to avoid battery low problems.
   The Restore from iTunes Backup option allows you to transfer music, photos and apps.

# How to Set Up As New

If this is your first iPhone and there is no need to transfer any data from any iDevices, simply follow these steps. First, you have to use your iCloud account.

1. **Tap Set Up As New**

   Under Apps & Data screen, select Set Up As New.

2. **Sign in with iCloud Apple ID**

   In order to use iCloud, iTunes and App Store, you need to sign in with your Apple ID. To sign in with your existing Apple ID, simply enter your email address and password. You can tap Use different Apple IDs for iCloud & iTunes if that is the set up that you want.

3. **Create an Apple ID**

   You can create an Apple ID right away for free or you can tap Skip This Step if you wish to continue later. You can create an Apple ID anytime you want to from the Settings app.

## 4. Agree to Terms and Conditions

Tap Agree to Apple's Terms and Conditions. Tap again to confirm your agreement.

## 5. Set up Apple Pay and iCloud Keychain

If you signed in with your Apple ID, you will be prompted to set up iCloud Drive, Apple Pay as well as iCloud Keychain.

Apple Pay is the Apple's Touch ID-based option for payment while iCloud Keychain is for saving and syncing all your passwords from all your devices.

## 6. Set Up Siri

The next interface that will appear is Siri. You can Set Up Siri right away or you can choose to Turn On Siri Later.

## 7. Choose Your Click

You can select the way of how your Home button will respond whenever you press it. Simply try all three and choose your preferred option. Simply tap Next once you are done. You can also skip this step and customize your Home button click later.

## 8. Display Zoom

The last step is to choose how you want to view your iPhone 7. Zoomed view allows you to see bigger controls, apps and texts while the Standard option is the normal view.

Simply tap **Get Started** to start using your brand new iPhone 7.

# How to Move Data from Android

Before you start, make sure that your Android device has Wi-Fi turned on. Connect your iPhone 7 and Android device in to power. Also check if your iOS device will have enough space for all the data that you wish to move from your Android device.

1. **Select Move Data from Android**

   Under Apps & Data screen, tap Move Data from Android option.

2. **Launch Move to iOS app**

   Open Move to iOS app on your Android device then tap Continue. Read and Agree to the terms and conditions the tap Next.

3. **Wait for Ten-digit of Six-digit Code**

   On your iPhone, tap Continue from Move from Android screen and wait for a code. If you received an alert on your Android device saying that the internet connection is weak, you can simply disregard it.

## 4. Enter the Code

Once you received your code, you can enter it on your Android device. Transfer Data screen will be displayed.

## 5. Select the Content

Choose the files you want to move from your Android device to your iPhone 7 then tap Next. A loading bar will appear on your iPhone and wait for it to be completed even if an alert on your Android tells you that the transfer is finished. Depending on the amount of your files, it may take some time.

You can transfer your photos and videos, messages, contact numbers, calendars, web bookmarks, email accounts and other apps available on both App Store and Google Play from your Android device to iOS.

## 6. Set Up

Once the loading bar is complete, tap Done from your Android and tap Continue on your iPhone. Follow the steps on your screen to finish.

# Set Up Mail, Contacts and Calendars

You can easily set up your mail, contacts and calendars whether you are using iCloud, Gmail, Outlook or others.

## ❏ iCloud Mail, Contacts and Calendars

1. Open **Settings** app on your iPhone and tap **iCloud**.
2. Enter your existing iCloud email and password then tap **Sign In**.
3. If you want all your data to combine with your iCloud storage, tap **Merge**. If not, tap **Don't Merge**.

4. Tap the switches next to Mail, Contacts, Calendars and other apps you wish to sync. By default, iCloud's services are enabled.

## ❏ **Gmail, Google Calendar and Google Contacts on iPhone 7**

To add your Google account to your new device, go to Settings and tap Mail, or Contacts or Calendar. You can use the built-in iOS Mail app by following the steps below.

1. From your Home screen, open **Settings** app.
2. Select **Mail**, **Contacts** or **Calendar.**
3. Tap **Accounts** and select **Add Account**.
4. Tap **Google** and enter your log in information. Simply tap **Next** after completing each step.
5. Toggle on the switches next to all the Google services you wish to sync. If you have existing mail, calendars and contacts, you need to tap either **Keep on My Phone** or **Delete**.
6. Tap **Save** to finish.

## ❑ **Outlook Mail, Contacts and Calendar**

If you are using Microsoft Outlook, here is the step by step instruction to set up your mail, contacts and calendar.

1. Open **Settings** app.
2. Select **Mail**, **Contacts** or **Calendar**.
3. Tap **Accounts** and select **Add Account**.
4. Enter your Outlook username and password then tap **Sign In**.
5. Tap **Yes** to collect your information.
6. Toggle on the switches next to all services you want to enable.
7. Tap **Save** to finish.

iPhone automatically locks when the screen has not been touched for a minute or more. You can adjust the lock timing by going to Settings > Display & Brightness > Auto-Lock.

# 2

## MESSAGES, FACETIME AND CAMERA

● **Message: Experience Excellent Messaging**

iMessage is the Apple's built-in Messaging app which allows you to send SMS, photos, videos, sound as well as location instantly. The Apple's latest version of operating system which is iOS 10 introduced more awesome features to make your messaging experience better. There are bubble effects that you can include in your messages such as invisible ink, slam, gentle and loud. You can also enjoy screen effects which are fireworks, confetti, balloons and lasers.

# How to Add Bubble Effects on Messages

To use the effects on your messages, you need to tap the **up arrow** on the bottom of the screen or right next to your text message box.

1. Type your message.

2. Tap the **up arrow** for at least two seconds to bring you to awesome effects which are slam, loud, gentle and invisible ink.

3. You can check how the effects will appear by swiping up and down.

4. Tap the dot next to the name of the effect that you want to use.

5. Tap the **up arrow** to send your message with effect.

# How to Add Screen Effects on Messages

To add screen effects, tap the up arrow for at least two seconds then swipe from Bubble to Screen. This will show you screen effects which are balloons, lasers, fireworks, shooting stars and confetti.

# How to Send Digital Touch Messages

Digital Touch is a feature which allows you to send hand-drawn sketch, fireball, kiss, heartbeat or heartbreak.

1. On the left side of your text message box, tap the **arrow pointing to the right** (>) to open another set of cool effects.

2. You will see three icons which are the Camera, Digital Touch which looks like a heart and the button for syncing with third-party apps. Tap the **Digital Touch** icon. If you have started typing, it will be hidden until you tap the arrow to reveal the icons.

3. From here, you can see different effects that you can try. You can check out change the color of effects by tapping the circle on the left.

4. You can now draw your sketch or use one finger or two to create different effects like heartbeat.

5. Once finished, tap Send (blue up arrow).

## How to Send Handwriting Message

Even if you can make a sketch of your messages in Digital Touch, there is also an added feature which allows you to handwrite your message.

1. Open Messages app and rotate your device to landscape mode. This will show you handwriting screen.

2. You can select from **previously sent** handwritten messages or write your new message with your finger.

3. Once finished, tap **Done**. You can also add more text if you need then tap the up arrow to send.

If you have to delete the handwritten message, you can always cancel it with the X icon or delete it with backspace key.

# How to Enable Text Replacement and Keyboard Shortcuts

If you always need to type the same phrases or sentences all over again, you can always create keyboard shortcuts that will automatically transform into the whole phrase or sentences. This feature is beneficial since you no longer have to type everything all the time. For instance, instead of typing your whole address, you can make a short cut which will automatically enter your whole address.

1. Open **Settings** app from home screen.

2. Tap **General** and select **Keyboard**.

3. Tap **Text Replacement**.

4. Tap the (+) sign to create keyboard shortcut and text replacement.

5. In the Phrase field, enter the whole phrase. (Example: Be Right Back)

6. In the Shortcut field, enter the shortcut you want to be replaced by the whole phrase. (Example: brb)

7. Once finished, tap **Save**.

You can create more keyboard shortcuts for the phrases that you often use. There are already premade shortcuts available in your device such as "omw" which becomes "On my way" after pressing the space bar.

## How to Enable QuickType

QuickType feature predicts the words that you want to type. There is no need to type the whole word. After typing two letters, list of words will appear which you can just tap to use.

1. Open **Settings** app from home screen.

2. Tap **General** and go to **Keyboard**.

3. Toggle on **Predictive** feature.

# Connect with Family and Friends using FaceTime

Apple devices have built-in app for audio and video calls which is FaceTime. This allows you to connect with your family and friends who are also using Apple devices. Once you register the contact number or e-mail of the person you want to contact and this person is also using an Apple device such as iPhone or iPad, you can easily connect with the person via FaceTime.

Before you start, make sure that you are connected to internet. The person that you wish to call via FaceTime should also have an active connection.

## How to Turn On FaceTime

FaceTime is enabled automatically once you finished your startup process. However, if it is not activated, you can enable it manually.

1. Open **Setting** app from Home screen.
2. Tap **FaceTime**.

3. Tap to toggle on the switch beside FaceTime.

## ❏ How to Make Audio Call using FaceTime

You can use FaceTime app to make a regular call. Just make sure that you and the contact you wish to call have internet access.

1. From your Home screen, open **FaceTime** app.

2. Tap the name of the person you wish to call on the search bar.

3. Tap the **Phone** button which looks like a telephone to start the call.

## ❏ How to Make Video Call using FaceTime

1. From your Home screen, open **FaceTime** app.

2. Tap the name of the person you wish to call on the search bar.

3. Tap the **Video** button which looks like a camera.

## ❑ How to Block Contacts in FaceTime

You can also block contacts from FaceTime. Whether it is a prank caller or an annoying friend or your stalker, you can stop them from bothering you.

1. From your Home screen, open FaceTime app.

2. Search for the contact you wish to block then tap the information button (i).

3. Scroll down and tap Block this Caller.

4. Tap **Block Contact**.

## ❑ Register Another Email Addresses for FaceTime

1. Open **Settings** app from Home screen and tap FaceTime.

2. **Below You can be reached by FaceTime at** section, tap **Add Another Email...**

3. Type the email address you want to add.

4. Tap Back (< **Settings**).

## How to Turn off FaceTime

1. Open **Settings** app from Home screen.

2. Tap **FaceTime**.

3. Tap to toggle off the switch beside FaceTime.

## Enjoy the Advanced and Powerful Camera

The built-in Camera on iPhone 7 allows you to take true-life photos, videos, time-lapses, panoramas, slow motions and more. The camera of iPhone 7 as well as iPhone 7 plus are beyond all expectations. There are plenty of new features including 12 MP camera, 7MP FaceTime HD camera, optical image stabilization and quad-LED true tone flash.

The **optical image stabilization** feature decreases the amount of blur from handshake or motion. There is a sensor which helps the lens to stabilize the movement for up to 3x longer exposure than iPhone 6s.

iPhone 7 camera's **f/1.8 aperture** allows more light to the sensor to increase its ability to take amazing low-light photos. It has **Quad-Led True Tone flash** which is 50 percent brighter compared to iPhone 6s.

❑ **How to Access Camera Quickly**

There are many ways to open the Camera app. Aside from tapping the Camera app, here are the other options on how to access camera quickly:

- The iOS 10 **lock screen** has new gesture which allows faster access to camera.

  **Step 1:** Touch your lock screen.

  **Step 2:** Swipe your finger to the left to access camera.

- You can access the Camera from **Control Center**.

  **Step 1:** Swipe from the bottom of the screen to open Control Center.

**Step 2:** Tap the Camera button located on the bottom right.

**Step 3:** Hold the Camera button for a longer time to display different options which are Take Photo, Record Slo-Mo, Record Video and Take Selfie.

- You can use "**Hey Siri**" to open the Camera app and take photos, videos or selfie for you. All you need to do is to say the right command.

**Step 1:** Press and hold the Home button or say "Hey Siri" if you have turned on this feature.

**Step 2:** When Siri is activated, you can mentioned these phrases.

For photo mode:
- "Take a picture"
- "Take a Panoramic picture"
- "Take a square picture"

For video mode:
- "Take a video"
- "Take a Time-Lapse video"
- "Take a Slow-Motion video"

For selfie mode:
- "Take a selfie"

Step 3: Siri will launch the Camera app automatically. Now you take photos, videos or selfie by tapping the Circle button.

❏ **How to Take Live Photos**

Live photos are different from videos. It is a full 12 MP photo that can animate for 1.5 seconds. Live photos also work with iPhone SE, iPhone 6s, iPhone 6 Plus, iPhone 7, iPhone 7 plus and 9.7-inch iPad Pro. You can make your selfies live and powerful.

**Step 1:** Open the **Camera** app.

**Step 2:** Tap the **Live Photo** button. This looks like diffused rings. It should turn yellow once activated.

**Step 3:** Tap the **Circle** button to start your Live Photo.

## ❑ How to Lock Focus and Exposure

**Step 1:** Open the **Camera** app.

**Step 2:** Tap anywhere on the screen to select the part of the photo you wish to focus and expose.

**Step 3:** Tap and hold that area until AE/AF Lock banner appears on top of the screen.

**Step 4:** Tap the Circle or Shutter button to take a photo.

To unlock focus and exposure, simply tap anywhere.

## ❑ Bias Exposure

You can bias exposure to make photos darker or brighter.

**Step 1:** Open **Camera** app.

**Step 2:** Tap anywhere to enhance the focus point.

**Step 3:** Tap and hold the **Exposure** button which looks like a sun until you see a slider. This slider lets you make adjustments of the exposure.

**Step 4:** Simply drag the slider up or down to bias exposure. You can make your photos either brighter or even darker.

❑ **How to Use Grid Lines**

If you want some help from grid lines for taking pictures, you can enable grid lines from Settings app.

**Step 1:** Open **Settings** app.

**Step 2:** Scroll down and select **Photos & Camera**.

**Step 3:** Scroll down until you see the Camera section. Toggle on the switch of **Grid**.

# 3

# MUSIC, NOTES AND SIRI

## Listen to Millions of Songs with Music App

There are four ways to get music on your new iPhone 7. You can easily purchase music directly from the iTunes Store, use iTunes Match with a fee of £21.99 per year, use iCloud Music Library or Sync music from iTunes using your Mac or PC.

# How to Sync Music from iTunes on PC or Mac

1. Connect your device to your Mac or PC via lightning cable.

2. Launch **iTunes**.

3. Click your device located in the top-left of the screen.

4. Select **Music** from the sidebar.

5. Click **Sync Music**.

6. It will sync your whole music library. If you do not want to sync all the songs from your iTunes library, simply put ticks next to the Playlists, Albums, Genres and Artists.

7. Click **Apply**. All music that you selected will be synced to your device.

# How to Use Music App

1. Open **Music** app from home screen.

2. You will see many options below the screen. If you did not take the Apple Music subscription yet, you will see: Library, For You, Browse, Radio and Search.

3. Tap **Library** to stream the music you added on your iPhone. You can select from Playlists, Artists, Albums, Songs and Downloaded Music.

4. Tap any song to start. It will show you the **Now Playing** interface. Simply tap the left and right arrows to switch songs. You can also tap **Repeat** or **Shuffle** button located at the bottom.

## Subscribe to Apple Music

You can listen to almost all tracks in iTunes Store when you subscribe to Apple Music. You also get three months free trial. If you want to get a subscription, simply open the **Music** app and tap **For You**. Then tap **Start three Month Free Trial**. Another way to subscribe is from **Settings** app. Select **Music** then tap **Show Apple Music**.

## Access Your Notes Anytime, Anywhere

Notes app is one of the most used apps on iPhone. It allows you to type anything that you like. Now, you can also make sketches so you can save your visual ideas next to your texts. There are different format and styles that you can choose from. You can also use numbered and bulleted list when necessary.

Photos, videos, audio, website links, documents and locations can also be added in your Notes app so you can keep everything that you need accordingly. You can use Notes app for almost everything from work to your shopping list. You can take some notes on your iPhone and continue it later on your Mac.

## Create and Edit New Notes

1. Open **Notes** app.

2. Tap **Create New Note** button from the bottom right.

3. Tap the screen to show the keyboard and you can start to take down notes.

4. To create another note, simply tap the **New Note** button.

5. To edit existing notes, tap the note you wish to edit then tap anywhere to show the keyboard.

# Move a Note to a New Folder

If you have many notes and you want to organize them by creating folders, you can do it easily.

1. Open **Notes** app.

2. Tap the existing folder where your note is saved.

3. Tap **Edit** from the upper right beside the name of the folder.

4. Tap the circle next to your note then tap **Move to...** in the bottom.

5. Choose a folder where you wish to transfer your note to.

# How to Delete and Recover Deleted Notes

To delete a note, simply tap the note you wish to delete then tap the **Trashcan** button in the bottom. Another way is to tap the title of the note then swipe it to the left to show two options: Move and Delete. Tap **Delete**.

If you want to recover your deleted notes, go to list view screen and tap Back button to display a list of folders. Tap **Recently Deleted** and look for the note that you want to recover. Swipe it to the left and tap **Move** to transfer it back to your folder.

## Enable Notes Sync with iCloud

To sync your notes with iCloud, follow these steps:

1. Open **Settings** app on your iPhone or iPad.
2. Select **iCloud**.
3. Enter your email address and password. Tap **Sign in**.
4. Enable Notes sync. Make sure that it is green.

## Set Password on your Notes

You can set a password on your Notes to keep it private even when someone has to borrow your iDevice. There are two ways to lock your notes.

## Lock Notes from Notes app:

1. Open **Notes** app from Home screen.

2. Tap a note that you want to lock then tap the **Share** button.

3. Tap **Lock Note** option to lock it.

4. Enter your **Password** which you will use for all your notes in your iDevices. Enter your password again.

5. You can add a hint if necessary.

6. If you want to unlock your notes easier, you can switch to **Touch ID** which can unlock your notes using your fingerprint.

## Lock Notes from Settings app:

1. Open **Settings** app from home screen.

2. Tap **Notes**.

3. Tap **Password**.

4. Enter your **Password** which you will use for all your notes in your iDevices. Enter your password again.

5. You can add a hint if necessary.

6. If you want to unlock your notes easier, you can switch to **Touch ID** which can unlock your notes using your fingerprint.

*Note: The entire body of the note will not be visible when locked but the title is in order to make it easier for you to find them. To keep all information hidden, make sure to avoid any info in the title.*

## How to Change Password on Notes

Changing passwords can be necessary from time to time.

1. Open **Settings** app then tap **Notes**.

2. Tap **Password** then select **Change Password**.

3. Enter your **Old Password**.

4. Enter your **New Password** and enter your new password again to confirm.

5. You can add a hint if necessary.

6. Once finished, tap **Done**.

# How to Unlock Notes

Your locked notes will remain hidden except for the title. To unlock your notes, follow these steps:

1. Open **Notes** app from Home screen.
2. Tap the note you wish to unlock.
3. Tap **View Note** or the **Lock** icon.
4. Enter your password or use Touch ID if you activated this feature.

# Siri: Get More Things Done

Siri is one of the most awesome features of Apple devices. You can complete your tasks faster with the help of Siri. You can ask questions like the how's the weather, latest movies in Netflix, nearby restaurants, new songs, stocks and more. You can command Siri to call someone, set a reminder, turn on timer, play songs, make reservations, read mails, create notes and calculate. There are more things that Siri can do for you.

After the release of iOS 10, Siri has become smarter than ever which can do almost everything you command from simple opening of apps to searching of information. Whether you are driving or cooking, you can command your smartphone using your voice.

## How to Activate "Hey Siri"

You can command Siri without having to hold your iPhone by activating "Hey Siri" feature. This feature works when your device is connected to a power.

1. Open **Settings** app.
2. Tap **Siri**.
3. Turn on **Siri**.
4. Turn on **"Hey Siri"**.
5. Follow the onscreen instructions which will ask you to speak "Hey Siri" three times and "How's the weather today."

When your iPhone is connected to charger, you can simply say Hey Siri and the Siri interface will open automatically. You can dismiss Siri by saying "**see you later**" or just "**bye**."

## Siri Now Works for Other Apps

Siri is now integrated with other apps which means that there are more things that you can do easily. Siri works with these types of apps:

- Messaging
- CarPlay
- Ride booking
- VoIP calling
- Photo and Video
- Payment
- Workouts

You can ask Siri which apps can work. If the app does not, Siri will tell you, "I wish I could, but (name of the app) hasn't set that up with me yet."

Siri is also working in the background by giving suggestions. For instance, Siri can make a calendar event depending on the conversation in email or iMessage. If you ask someone if they want to go out for dinner, Siri can make suggestions of nearby restaurants. It also makes suggestions on keyboard which is known as the **QuickType** feature.

# 4

# PASSCODE AND TOUCH ID

**S**et Passcode on Your iPhone

Setting a passcode on your iPhone prevents anyone from unlocking your device as they need to enter numbers to unlock it first. This means that it will be hard for your friends or anyone to check your private photos, messages, health and financial information.

## How to Set Passcode

1. Open **Settings** app from home screen.
2. Select **Touch ID & Passcode**.
3. Tap **Turn Passcode On**.

4. Enter your passcode and re-enter passcode to confirm.

# Change Passcode

If you want to change passcode, you can always do so.

1. Open **Settings** app from home screen.

2. Select **Touch ID & Passcode**.

3. Enter your current passcode.

4. Select **Change Passcode**.

5. Re-enter your current passcode.

6. Enter your new passcode. Re-enter to confirm.

# How to Switch to Alphanumeric Passcode

If you prefer more complicated passcode but not long enough that you might not remember, alphanumeric can be your choice.

1. Open **Settings** app from home screen.

2. Select **Touch ID & Passcode**.

3. Enter your current passcode.

4. Tap **Change Passcode** and re-enter your current passcode.

5. Tap **Passcode Options** and select **Custom Alphanumeric Code**.

6. Enter your new alphanumeric password. Re-enter to confirm.

## How to Turn Passcode Off

It is recommended to keep your passcode on. If you need to turn passcode off, here's what to do.

1. Open **Settings** app from home screen.

2. Select **Touch ID & Passcode**.

3. Enter your current passcode.

4. Tap **Turn Passcode Off** and confirm.

5. Re-enter your passcode to turn off.

## Touch ID: More Convenient Way to Unlock Device

Touch ID is your device's sensor in the Home button to identify your fingerprint. This is one form of security which is more convenient than having to enter your passcode. Since you always use your iPhone, you will need to unlock it every now and then. Typing your password all the time can be inconvenient at times. Touch ID allows you to unlock your screen faster.

## ❑ **How to Set Up Touch ID**

During the initial set up, you were asked to register your fingerprint. You can also add more fingers any time you want to.

1. Open **Settings** app from home screen.

2. Tap **Touch ID & Passcode**.

3. Type your passcode to confirm. Entering passcode requires Touch ID and if you do not have it yet, you will be prompted to create.

4. Tap **Add a Fingerprint** button.

5. Place the **finger** you wish to register on **Home button** until it vibrates.

6. Raise your finger then put it back on Home button every time you feel the vibration.

7. When it prompts that it has finished the first step and requires peripheral data, tap **Continue**.

8. Put the edges of the finger you wish to register on the Home button. Leave it until it vibrates.

9. Raise your finger then put it back on Home button. Repeat using the other edge of your finger until the entire surface is registered.

10. Once finished, tap **Continue**.

You can add more fingers by repeating all the steps above. You can allow your family members' fingerprint or someone you really trust.

## ❑ How to Rename Touch ID Fingerprints

You can put names on your fingerprint so you would not have to identify which fingers are already registered. For instance, you can name it "right thumb" if you registered your right thumb.

1. Open **Settings** app.

2. Tap **Touch ID & Passcode**.

3. Enter your passcode when prompted.

4. Tap the finger you wish to rename.

5. Enter the name that is more convenient for you to identify.

5. Once finished, tap **Done.**

## ❑ How to Delete Touch ID Fingerprint

If you allowed someone to gain access to your iPhone for a short period of time and there is no need for that person to have an access to your device, you can easily delete their fingerprint.

1. Open **Settings** app from home screen.
2. Select **Touch ID & Passcode.**
3. Enter your passcode when asked.
4. Select the **fingerprint** you wish to delete.
5. Tap **Delete Fingerprint** then tap **Done** to finish.

## ❑ How to Disable Touch ID for iPhone Unlock

Touch ID allows you to unlock your device faster. If you prefer typing alphanumeric for stronger password, you can disable Touch ID.

1. Open **Settings** app from home screen.

2. Select **Touch ID & Passcode**.

3. Enter your passcode when asked.

4. Toggle off **iPhone Unlock**.

## ❏ How to Disable Touch ID for Apple Pay

Touch ID is required for Apple Pay. If you prefer to enter your passcode, simply disable Touch ID for Apple Pay.

1. Open **Settings** app.

2. Select **Touch ID & Passcode**.

3. Enter your passcode when asked.

4. Toggle off **Apple Pay**.

## ❏ How to Disable Touch ID for iTunes and App Store

If you prefer typing your password on iTunes and App Store than using Touch ID, you can also turn it off.

1. Open **Settings** app.
2. Select **Touch ID & Passcode**.
3. Enter your passcode when asked.
4. Toggle off **iTunes & App Store**.

## ❑ Cases when Touch ID Turns Off Automatically

There are cases that Touch ID turns off automatically to secure your files and information.

- When Touch ID has not been used in forty eight hours.
- When your devices has been reset or rebooted.
- When fingerprint is not recognized five times in a row.
- When passcode has not been used to unlock in 6 days.
- When a remote lock has been sent using Find My iPhone.

You will have to enter your passcode again to activate Touch ID.

# 5

# 3D TOUCH AND AIRPLAY

**M**ake Quick Actions with 3D Touch

3D Touch allows you to press the display in order to do more with your games and other apps. You can move around and complete tasks even faster. You can activate trackpad mode using 3D touch and also animate your live photos.

## Home Screen Actions with 3D Touch

There are many actions available from your home screen. All you have to do is to press firmly.

1. From Home screen, press firmly on an **icon** you wish to open quick actions for.

2. A list of actions will be displayed. Tap the action that you need.

## Switch Apps with 3D Touch

You can easily switch apps using 3D touch.

1. Press firmly on the left side of your screen.

2. Swipe to the right to see previous apps and swipe more to the right to show fast app switcher.

3. Swipe to the app you wish to open then tap that app.

## Check and Clear Notifications with 3D Touch

You can check and interact with your notifications using 3D touch. From lock screen, simply swipe to the right to see Notification Center.

1. Press a notification you want to interact with.

2. You can type and interact with the notification.

3. To disregard the notification, simply tap the X button.

3D touch also allows you to clean your Notification Center by deleting all notifications. To do this:

1. Press the **X** button on top of the notifications.

2. Tap **Clear All Notifications**.

## Peek and Pop

3D Touch allows you to peek and pop messages, automatic links and website links. Peek allows you to perform certain actions without opening the app.

1. Press the link or item you wish to peek at.

2. The link or item will be highlighted while the rest of your screen will become blurred.

3. To peek at the item or link, simply press firmly.

4. Once finished, you can let go to release the peek.

5. For more actions, simply swipe up from the item or link to show the list.

6. Select the action you wish to perform.

To pop a message and show it in your entire screen:

1. Press the message to peek.

2. To make it pop, press longer.

3. To go back to the previous app, simply tap the Back button or press hard on the left side of the screen then swipe to the right.

## How to Customize 3D Touch

If you want to change the sensitivity level of your 3D touch, it is easy to do so.

1. Open **Settings** app from home screen.

2. Select **General**.

3. Tap **Accessibility** and select **3D Touch**.

4. There are three levels that you can choose from: **light, medium** and **firm**.

5. Select your desired sensitivity level.

# How to Turn Off 3D Touch

If you prefer to disable 3D touch, you can easily do so.

1. Open **Settings** app from home screen.

2. Select **General**.

3. Tap **Accessibility** and select **3D Touch**.

4. Toggle off 3D Touch.

# AirPlay: Stream Photos, Videos, Movies and Music to Apple TV

AirPlay can only be used when there is an active connection. Once you connect all your devices that are compatible with AirPlay to the same internet connection, you can stream your videos or music on Apple TV or AirPlay Speaker. You can enjoy movies on bigger screen or mirror your entire iPhone screen.

❑ **How to Use AirPlay Video**

1. To use AirPlay, open **Control Center** by swiping up from the bottom of the screen.

2. Tap the **AirPlay** button.

3. Tap to confirm and your iPhone 7 will start searching for an Apple TV.

4. If the Apple TV you want to use has different network from your iPhone, it will show a code which you have to enter on your iPhone.

## ❑ How to Stop AirPlay Video

1. To end AirPlay video, open **Control Center** by swiping up from the bottom of the screen.

2. Tap the **AirPlay** button.

3. Tap **Turn Off AirPlay Mirroring**.

## ❑ How to Use AirPlay Audio

1. To stream your music to Apple TV or AirPlay speakers, open **Control Center** by swiping up from the bottom of the screen.

2. Swipe to the left to open **Now Playing** screen.

3. Select **Audio Destination** and choose the device where you want to stream your music.

## ❏ How to Stop AirPlay Audio

1. To stop AirPlay audio, simply go to **Control Center** by swiping up from the bottom of the screen.

2. Swipe from right to left top open **Now Playing** screen.

3. Tap the **Audio Destination** button and select iPhone to discontinue AirPlay.

# 6

# TWO-FACTOR AUTHENTICATION AND ICLOUD KEYCHAIN

## Two-Factor Authentication for Additional Security

The security of your information is one of the things that have to be given importance. For more security of your iCloud account and your Apple ID, Apple released two-factor authentication feature. This feature provides an extra layer of protection for all your accounts. You can only use this feature only on the devices that you trust so there is no way other people can gain access to your information.

When two-factor authentication feature is enabled, you will have to enter your password plus a six-digit verification code when logging in to a different or new device. This only means that if someone tries to sign in your account from their devices, they cannot succeed even if they were able to know your first password.

## How Two-Factor Authentication Works

Two-factor authentication only works on all devices that you trusted such as your iPhone, iPad and your Mac. If you have to sign in on your new device, you will need to enter a six-digit code which will be displayed on your trusted devices. First, you need to enter the six-digit code on your trusted devices to confirm that the new device is also trusted. This means that your first password is not enough to get your account. Two-factor authentication can make your information double secured.

# How to Turn On Two-Factor Authentication

1. Open **Settings** app from home screen.

2. Select **iCloud**.

3. Tap **Apple ID** and enter your password when asked.

4. Select **Password & Security**.

5. Enable **Two-Factor Authentication**.

6. Tap **Continue** and follow the given instructions from your screen.

Once the two-factor authentication is on, you will need to verify yourself when signing in to iCloud or Apple ID page. You also need to confirm when making purchases from iBooks, App Store and iTunes using new devices. iMessage, Game Center and FaceTime are also covered by two-factor authentication.

# Keep Passwords and Usernames with iCloud Keychain

You can keep your usernames and passwords for Safari, credit card and Wi-Fi network up to date for all your iOS devices and Mac. It is secured with 256-bit AES encryption. iCloud Keychain can be used with Safari Password Generator and AutoFill. You can use AutoFill to let your device enter your account information automatically. To keep your information secured, you have to set a passcode when enabling iCloud Keychain and AutoFill.

1. To set up **iCloud Keychain**, open **Settings** app from home screen.

2. Tap **iCloud** then select **Keychain**.

3. Toggle on **iCloud Keychain**.

4. Follow the instructions onscreen.

During the set up, you need to create a security code to authorize your other devices in using iCloud Keychain.

# 7

# REMINDERS AND APP STORE

**N**ever Forget with Reminder App

You can always ask Siri to make a reminder for you. But if you prefer to manually create your reminder and organize everything yourself, it is easy to navigate the Reminder app. You can also choose the priorities of your reminders.

## How to Create a Reminder

1. Open the **Reminders** app.
2. Tap the (+) icon to create a reminder.

3. Enter your reminder on the space provided then tap (**i**).

4. You can enable either "**Remind me on a day**" or "**Remind me at a location**". Remind me at a location gives you a reminder when you arrive or leave from your chosen location.

5. Choose the **priority** of your reminder. You can select from one exclamation mark to three exclamation marks.

6. To add notes on your reminder, simply tap **Notes** under Priority.

7. Tap **Done** to save your reminder.

## Download Apps and Games from App Store

There are millions of games and apps that you can download to your device. You can download Facebook app directly to your device so it is just one tap away. Edit your documents anytime and anywhere. Play millions of games whether online or offline. There are many apps to discover. The categories of apps in App Store are:

- Books
- Business
- Catalogues
- Education
- Entertainment
- Finance
- Food & Drink
- Games

- Health & Fitness
- Kids
- Lifestyle
- Magazines & Newspapers

- Medical
- Music
- Navigation
- News
- Photo & Video
- Productivity
- Shopping
- Social Networking
- Sports
- Travel
- Utilities
- Weather

# How to Search and Download Games and Apps

Once you have an Apple ID, you can make start downloading games and other apps from App Store.

1. Open **App Store**.

2. Tap the **Search** button at the bottom of your screen.

3. Enter the name of app that you want to download.

4. Tap **Search**. When the results appeared, tap **Get** if the app is free or the **price** if it is paid app then tap **Install**.

## Update Your Apps

Developers always release new updates to keep the apps glitches-free. To check if there are new updates:

1. Open **App Store**.

2. Tap **Updates**.

3. All apps with new updates are available to install. Simply tap the **Update** button of the apps you wish to update.

## Update Apps Automatically

You can update your apps automatically without having to open App Store.

1. Open **Settings** app.

2. Select **iTunes & App Store**.

3. Tap the switch next to **Updates** under Automatic Downloads. This will automatically update your apps when connected to internet.

From here, you can also enable automatic downloads for Books & Audiobooks, Apps and Music.

## How to Disable Updates When Using Cellular

To avoid using cellular data from updating apps, it is best turn off automatic update for Cellular Data.

1. Open **Settings** app from home screen.

2. Select **iTunes & App Store**.

3. Toggle off the switch next to **Use Cellular Data**.

# 8

# PERSONALIZE, AIRDROP AND BATTERY .

## Personalize Your iPhone

You can easily personalize your iPhone.

## Arrange Apps

To arrange your apps, simply tap and hold the app from your home screen until all apps are jiggling. Drag the app that you wish to move. You can also transfer your apps from different home screen by dragging the app to the edge of the screen.

To delete apps from your home screen, tap the **X** button on top of the app. You can also delete some of the built-in Apple apps such as Calculator, Calendar, Compass, Contacts, FaceTime, Home, Podcasts, Reminders, Stocks, Voice Memos, Watch, Weather and more.

You can create a folder of your apps by dragging one app to another app. Tap the name of the folder to change its name. To save your app arrangement, simply tap the Home button.

## Change Wallpaper

To change your wall paper, go to Settings > Wallpaper > Choose a New Wallpaper. You can also use your own image for your wallpaper.

To set a Live Photo as your wall paper for lock screen, go to Settings > Wallpaper > Choose New Wallpaper. From there, tap Live and choose your live photo.

When you are on your lock screen, you can press to watch your live photo.

## Adjust Screen Brightness

Low brightness or auto-brightness feature can conserve your battery life. You can use Night Shift to make your screen warmer during the night. To adjust the brightness of your screen, go to Settings then tap Display & Brightness. Drag the slider to adjust. Screen brightness can also be adjusted from the Control Center.

## Change iPhone Name

If you want to use your change the name of your iPhone, go to Settings and tap General. Select About. Tap Name.

## Share Your Files with AirDrop

AirDrop allows you to share your files such as photos, videos, locations, websites and other items with other devices running iOS 7 or later. AirDrop requires an active internet connection and Bluetooth to transfer the files. You also have to sign in to your iCloud.

To share files using AirDrop, simply select the photo or video you wish to share. Tap the share button then select the name of the person you want to share the files with.

To receive AirDrop files from others, all you have to do is to enable AirDrop and Bluetooth from Control Center. Once the request arrives, tap Accept.

## How to Enhance iPhone 7 Battery Life

The battery life of iPhone 7 as well as iPhone 7 plus is already improved. It is longer than its predecessors. iPhone 7 is packed with new awesome features with enhanced performances. It includes improved camera features. If you want to make the battery life of your device longer, these are some tips that you can do.

## ❑ Turn on Low Power Mode

The iPhone 7 comes with a feature Low Power Mode which can help your battery to last even longer. Low Power Mode prompts automatically once your battery reaches 20% and you can enable it by then. But if you want to turn it on even if you still have 100%, you may do so.

When Low Power Mode is on, it stops all apps running in the background. It also stops fetching new data to conserve the battery.

1. Launch **Settings** app.
2. Tap **Battery**.
3. Turn on **Low Power Mode**.

## ❑ Turn On Auto Brightness

Auto Brightness feature adjusts the screen brightness automatically. When your surroundings are bright, your screen will become brighter so you can see your screen well. Once it is night time or you are already in bed, your screen automatically lowers its brightness which can help in conserving your device's battery life.

1. Open **Settings** app.
2. Tap **Display & Brightness.**
3. Toggle on **Auto Brightness.**

## ❑ **Disable Push Notification**

Push notifications for mails and calendar contribute to draining your battery life fast. You can disable this feature if you do not need push notification. You can always open your app to check for new data.

1. Open **Settings** app from home screen.

2. Tap **Notifications.**

3. Toggle off **Push** notifications for apps that you do not need Push.

## ❑ **Disable Location Services**

When not using location services, it is best to turn it off. Location service is a great feature and can consume battery life as well. You can always turn it back on when needed such as when using Google Maps or Waze.

1. Launch **Settings** app from home screen.

2. Select **Privacy**.

3. Toggle off **Location Services**.

When using Google Maps or other apps that require location, you can easily turn it back on by repeating the same steps then toggle on Location Services. Once finished with the feature, turn it back off to conserve the battery life of your device.

## ❑ Turn Off Background App Refresh

Your device will keep the apps running in the background. Even if you are using a different app, the previous apps you used and you did not close will continue consuming your battery. It collects data and information in the background in order to keep you updated even without having to open the app. With feature on, there is no need to refresh the apps. However, if you need to conserve your battery, it is best to turn this feature off. To turn off background app refresh feature:

1. Open **Settings** app from home screen.

2. Tap **General**.

3. Scroll down and select **Background App Refresh**.

4. Turn off the switch to discontinue apps in the background from collecting new data.

# 9

# BASIC TROUBLESHOOTI NG SOLUTIONS

P**erform Basic Troubleshooting Solutions**

If you are experiencing some problems with your iPhone 7, learn what to do:

## Touch ID Stopped Working

If Touch ID stopped working, follow these steps:

1. Go to **Settings** and tap **Touch ID & Passcode**.

2. Enter your passcode. Toggle **off** the switches next to iTunes & Apple Store and Apple Pay.

3. **Reboot** your iPhone and wait for few minutes before turning it back on.

4. Turn **on** your device and go back to Settings.

5. Toggle **on** the switches next to iTunes & Apple Store and Apple Pay.

The alternative solution is to delete fingerprints that you registered. Follow these steps:

1. Open **Settings** app and select **Touch ID & Passcode**.

2. Turn **off** each item then tap **Delete Fingerprint**.

3. **Add A Fingerprint** again and turn back **on** all items.

## iMessage Not Working

iMessage only works when there is an active connection such as Wi-Fi and 3G network. Make sure that your device is connected to internet when using iMessage. Here are some solutions that you can do:

1. **Turn off iMessage**. Do this by going to Settings > Messages > iMessage. Turn it back on after few minutes and make sure you are connected to 3G or Wi-Fi.

2. **Reboot your device**. Press and hold down Sleep/Wake button until the slider appears. Swipe the slider to turn off. Wait for few seconds before turning your devices on.

3. **Toggle on and off Airplane mode**. Go to Settings > Airplane Mode.

4. **Reset Network Settings**. To reset network settings, open Settings > General > Reset > Reset Network Settings. After resetting, you will need to connect your device again to Wi-Fi and enter the password.

# iMessage Effects Not Working

iMessage is packed with new features. There are bubble and screen effects that you can use to improve your iMessaging experience. If the effects are not working, learn what to do.

Turn off Reduce Motion. Go to Settings app and tap General. Select Accessibility and look for Reduce Motion. Make sure that Reduce Motion feature is off to enable bubble and screen effects on iMessage.

# iMessage Handwriting Feature Not Working

You can easily access handwriting screen in Messages app by tilting your device to landscape mode. If it does not appear, simply tap Handwriting feature button which looks like a small loop. This will show the handwriting space. To go back to keyboard, simply tap the keyboard button.

# Device Cannot Connect to Wi-Fi

If experiencing Wi-Fi grayed out, you can try some of the solutions below:

1. **Disable Wi-Fi Settings.** Go to Settings, tap Privacy and select Location Services. Tap System Services then look for Wi-Fi Networking. Turn off Wi-Fi Networking.

2. **Restart your iPhone**. Press and hold down Sleep/Wake button until the slider appears. Swipe the slider to turn off your device. Turn your device back on and try to connect to Wi-Fi.

3. **Reset Network Settings**. To reset network settings, open Settings > General > Reset > Reset Network Settings. After resetting, you will need to connect your device again to Wi-Fi and enter the password.

# Apps Not Producing Sounds

If there are no sounds when opening your apps, here are the solutions to fix the issue.

1. **Check Mute Switch**. The mute switch is on the left side of the device. Make sure that the switch is not showing orange. If it shows orange, it means your device is muted.

2. **Turn off Bluetooth**. Your device can still be connected to Bluetooth speaker or headset. Switch off Bluetooth by swiping up from the bottom of the screen to open Control Center. Turn Bluetooth off.

3. **Disable Do Not Disturb**. Open Control Center and tap the moon sign to turn off Do Not Disturb feature. When this feature is on, it prevents your device from making any sound.

4. **Check Volume Setting.** The volume setting of your device can be on zero which results to your apps

not producing sounds. Open the app you are having problems with and press the volume button at the side of your device.

5. **Reset All Settings**. To reset, open Settings > General > Reset > Reset All Settings.

## How to Remove "Press Home Button to Unlock"

If you do not want to press the Home button to unlock your device, you can enable Rest Finger to Open. You do not actually press the Home button. It is just a haptic feedback which gives the feeling of pressing the button. To disable the haptic feedback, go to **Settings** > **General** > **Accessibility** > **Home Button** then toggle on **Rest Finger to Open**.

## FaceTime Not Working

FaceTime works when there is an active connection. Make sure that your device is connected to Wi-Fi or

3G to use it. If it still does not work, try some of the solutions below.

1. **Get the Latest Update of iOS**. Make sure that you have installed the new update of iOS. Go to Settings, tap General and select Software Update. If your device is up to date, check more solutions below.

2. **Check if FaceTime is on**. Make sure that FaceTime is toggled on in Settings. To check, open Settings app and scroll down to FaceTime. Make sure that it is on or it is green.

3. **Reactivate your account**. Open Settings and tap FaceTime. Turn it off and wait for a minute before turning it back on. Enter your Apple ID and password.

4. **Reboot your device.** To reboot your device, hold down the Sleep/Wake button together with the Volume down button until the Apple logo appears. Once on, try to connect to FaceTime again.

5. **Use Same Apple ID**. Make sure that your Apple ID is the same as your FaceTime account. To check, open Settings app and tap FaceTime.

6. **Toggle on and off Airplane mode**. Go to Settings and toggle on and off Airplane Mode.

7. **Reset Network Settings**. To reset network settings, open Settings > General > Reset > Reset Network Settings. After resetting, you will need to connect your device again to Wi-Fi and enter the password.

## Keyboard Landscape Mode Not Functioning

You can easily switch to landscape mode on keyboard when you tilt your device. If landscape mode does not appear, here are some solutions that you can do.

1. **Turn your device off and on**. Once on, go to Messages app and tilt your keyboard. Landscape mode should appear instantly.

2. **Disable Turn to Listen**. Another solution that can be done is to go to Settings and tap Messages. Turn off Raise to Listen.

# Bluetooth Not Working with Other Devices

If having problems with Bluetooth, know what to do:

1. **Turn Bluetooth off**. Go to Settings and turn off Bluetooth. Reboot your device by holding the Sleep/Wake button and Volume down button until the Apple logo appears. When your device is on, turn Bluetooth on and connect it to your other device.

2. **Forget This Device**. Another solution is to forget the device you want to connect. Go to Settings and tap Bluetooth. Tap the information button (i) next to the device name. Tap "Forget This Device" and confirm. Try to pair again with the device and it should work.

3. **Reset Network Settings**. To reset network settings, open Settings > General > Reset > Reset Network Settings. After resetting, you will need to connect your device again to Wi-Fi and enter the password.

iPhone 7 is one of the most advanced gadgets available in the market today. It is packed with cool features that can make your daily tasks easier while enjoying your smartphone experience. It is your all-in-one device which allows you to take real-life photos, connect to your family and friends anytime and anywhere, install apps that you need and more. You can easily command Siri to make actions for you.

# Conclusion

I hope this guide has helped you understand more about the phone in details. Wishing you all the best and good luck!

# iOS 10

*An Ultimate Guide to Apple's Latest iOS Version*

# INTRODUCTION

This book contains all the new features and information that you need about the latest launch of Apple iOS 10. It also contains detailed instructions on how you can get the best experience from the latest version of operating system.

# 1

# LOCK SCREEN AND HOME SCREEN

Apple users who upgraded their device to iOS 10 finally have the chance to send stickers in iMessage app, add personal touch in their messages, wake up device by raising, experience smarter Siri and more. 3D touch is available for checking notifications and allows you to make actions from notifications such as replying to messages.

Notifications are also easy to clear and control center has an additional area for controlling music.

The latest operating system of Apple introduces new features that can make your iPhone, iPad or iPod more efficient. Siri, the iOS's virtual assistant, is constantly updated. With iOS 10, you can send money or get a cab as Siri is now able to assist you with third party apps.

## Update Your iDevice

If you have not updated your iDevice, it is already the right time you download and install the latest version. To get the latest update, all you have to do is to tap the **Settings** app, select **General** and tap **Software Update**. If you have installed iOS 9, the new update should appear.

Simply tap **Download and Install** to continue. It is required to connect your device to an active connection in order to download the update. The battery should also have sufficient power or at least connected to a charger. Read and accept the **Terms**

**and Conditions** and wait for the download and installation to finish.

You can also update your device using **iTunes**. Connect your device to PC or Mac. Launch iTunes and click the name of your device. You will see **Check for Update**. Click that and iTunes will search for the latest update.

Updating is easy and completely free. iOS 10 is compatible with the following devices:

| | | |
|---|---|---|
| iPhone 7 | iPhone 5c | iPad 4$^{th}$ generation |
| iPhone 7 Plus | iPhone 5 | iPad mini 4 |
| iPhone 6s | iPad Pro 12.9-inch | iPad mini 3 |
| iPhone 6s Plus | iPad Pro 9.7-inch | iPad mini 2 |
| iPhone 6 | iPad Air 2 | iPod touch 6$^{th}$ generation |
| iPhone 6 Plus | iPad Air | |
| iPhone SE | | |
| iPhone 5s | | |

Features and apps vary depending on the model that you have. Other factors that affect the features are the location, carrier and language.

# What's New in Apple's Latest iOS 10 Version

iOS 10 takes all previous features and new ones to the next level. It has better designs, more consistent and very neat. It offers additional security for your personal information and it is more intelligent than ever. The new Home app allows you to control all your home accessories with only one tap. 3D Touch is also even more powerful and more dominating.

## Lock Screen in iOS 10

Lock screen is the first page you see when you wake your device up. You can also get to the lock screen when you press the On/Off button or the Home button. It displays new messages, notifications and more. Lock screen also keeps your device secured from unauthorized users.

The lock screen of all previous versions of iOS display the date and time, wallpaper and allows you to "Slide to Unlock" your device. Since the first version, new features have been added such as accessing the Notification Center, shortcut to access Camera and more.

iOS 10 has changed the appearance and added new features on Lock screen. It also changed the way you unlock your device. You can see your notifications from lock screen and you can perform quick actions. Once you are familiar with the new functions, you can achieve a much better experience.

## How to Unlock Your Device

One of the biggest changes in iOS 10 is the way you unlock it. The famous "Slide to Unlock" gesture is no longer applicable. Unlocking your device will take you to Home screen or to the last app that you opened. Your device is can be secured with a Touch ID or Passcode.

If you have not set up the Touch ID or Passcode:

1. You can unlock your device by simply tapping the **Home** button.

If you have already set up a Passcode:

1. Press the **Home** button.
2. Enter your passcode.

If you have already set up a Touch ID:

1. Place the finger you registered on the **Home** button.
2. Press the Home button.

## How to Set up a Passcode

Your device will ask you to set a passcode during the set up process. If you skipped that step or you turned it off in the meantime, you can always set it up again.

1. Open **Settings** app from Home screen.
2. Select **Touch ID & Passcode**.
3. Select **Turn Passcode On**.
4. If you prefer to have custom alphanumeric code, custom numeric code or 6-digit numeric code, tap **Passcode Options**.

5. Enter your passcode.

6. Re-enter to confirm.

# How to Change Passcode Time Requirement

You can set a period of time to keep your device unlock.

1. Open **Settings** app from Home screen.

2. Select **Touch ID & Passcode**.

3. Enter your passcode.

4. Tap Require Passcode.

5. Select from the choices:

- Immediately

- After 1 minute

- After 5 minutes

- After 15 minutes

- After 1 hour

- After 4 hours

## How to Set up Touch ID

Touch ID is the fingerprint identity sensor in the newer models of iOS. It is a biometric security that is easier and more convenient than having to enter a passcode. Touch ID is built inside the Home button and every time you use it, the fingerprint recognition also enhances. Over time, it can work in any finger angles.

These are the cases when Touch ID automatically turns off to secure your information:

- If a fingerprint is not recognized five times in a row. You will have to enter your passcode to enable it again.
- If your device has been reset or rebooted. You will have to enter your passcode to enable it again.

- If Touch ID has not been used in two days. You will have to enter your passcode to enable it again.
- If passcode has not been used to unlock in 6 days and Touch ID has not been used to unlock in 6 hours. You will have to enter your passcode to enable it again.
- If a remote lock has been sent using Find my iPhone. You will have to enter your passcode to enable it again.

**To set up Touch ID:**

1. Open **Settings** app from Home screen.
2. Select **Touch ID & Passcode**.
3. Enter your passcode if asked. Touch ID also requires a passcode and if you have not yet set it up, you will be asked to set it up.
4. Tap the **Add a Fingerprint** button.
5. Place the finger you wish to register on the Home button. Let it sit until you feel a vibration.

6. Raise your finger and put it back on the Home button. Repeat this step every time you feel the buzz.

7. Touch ID will alert you that the first step has been completed. It will require a peripheral data. Simply tap **Continue**.

8. Put the edges of the finger you wish to register on the Home button. Let it sit until you feel a vibration.

9. Raise your finger and put it back down. Repeat it in different edge until the entire surface of the finger has been registered.

10. Tap **Continue**.

You can register up to five fingerprints. Simply repeat the step-by-step instructions for all the fingers that you wish to register. You can also include members of your family or trusted friend.

# How to Access Camera from Lock Screen

The new iOS 10 Lock screen offers a different way to access the Camera interface. It is much easier as you do not have to try many times just to tap the small camera icon.

1. Get to **Lock screen** page by pressing either the On/Off button or Home button.
2. Swipe your finger to the left to access Camera.

# How to Access Today View Widgets from Lock Screen

Widgets have been combined with the recommendations of Siri and you can access them easier even in Lock screen.

1. Press **On/Off** button or **Home** button to get in to Lock screen page.
2. Swipe your finger to the right to view widgets.

## To add/remove widgets:

3. Tap the Edit button at the bottom of the screen.

4. Under the More Widgets, tap the **plus** (+) icon next to the name of the widgets you wish to add.

   To remove widgets, simply tap the **minus** (-) button next to the name of the widgets you want to remove. Tap **Remove**.

## To arrange your widgets in specific order:

5. Tap and hold the three horizontal lines at the right side of the widgets and drag it on the place where you want them to be.

6. Once you are finished, tap **Done**.

# How to Access Notification Center from Lock Screen

The Notification Center can be accessed easily even from the Lock screen.

1. Simply tap the bezel from the top of the screen.

2. Swipe down to display the notification center.

You can also swipe right to enter the Today View from Notification Center.

## How to Access Control Center from Lock Screen

Control Center allows you to quickly turn on and off Airplane mode, Wi-Fi, Bluetooth, Do not disturb and Rotation lock. It also allows you to adjust the screen brightness and volume. You can also open flashlight, calculator, timer and camera through control center.

1. Touch the bezel from the bottom of the screen.
2. Swipe your finger up to display control center.

iOS 10 control center has another tray where you can see the streaming music. Simply swipe your finger to the left to enter the next tray.

## How to Access Siri from Lock Screen

iPhone 6s, iPhone 6s Plus, iPhone SE, iPad Pro 9.7-inch devices allow you to activate Siri even from a far. Voice activation does not work if the device is in Low Power Mode.

1. To activate Siri, simply say "Hey, Siri!"
2. Another way to activate Siri is to press and hold down the Home button.

Siri can do more things. It is also smarter than ever. You can ask Siri to get directions, make phone calls, and send new texts and emails and more.

## Home Screen in iOS 10

There are many built-in apps that you do not really use and take up some space of your screen. The best thing that you can do is to hide them by keeping them all together in a box. The latest version now allows you to **delete built-in apps** that you do not use just like how you delete apps that you downloaded from App Store.

Simply touch and hold down any app until all apps start to shake. Tap the **X** button to delete the app. However, not all built-in apps can be deleted. But this saved you more space not only on your Home screen but also in your storage.

The Home screen is also enhanced with 3D Touch. When you press firmly on any app, you can see more options or actions that you can choose from. You can also press firmly on bundled apps actions involved among all the apps inside.

# 2

# RAISE TO WAKE, NOTIFICATION CENTER, CONTROL CENTER AND SIRI

## Raise to Wake on iPhone

R iOS 10 allows you to turn on the display of your iPhone when you pick it up.

It allows you to see your notification quickly without having to press any button. Raise to Wake feature only works on iPhone SE, iPhone 6s Plus, iPhone 6s, iPhone 7 Plus and iPhone 7.

## How to Enable Raise to Wake Feature

Raise to Wake feature is on by default once you installed the iOS 10. If it is still not enabled, you can also turn it on manually.

1. Open **Settings** app from home screen.
2. Select **Display & Brightness**.
3. Turn on the switch beside **Raise to Wake**. Make sure that it is green.

When this feature is on, your iPhone will automatically wake up whenever you pick it up from a flat surface. There is no need to press the On/Off button or Home button.

## How to Disable Raise to Wake

You can easily disable the Raise to Wake feature if you do not like the automatic display whenever you lift your iPhone.

1. Open **Settings** app from home screen.
2. Select **Display & Brightness**.
3. Turn off the switch beside **Raise to Wake**.

## Notification Center in iOS 10

The Notification center on iOS 10 has been redesign creatively and it allows you to make quick actions. With the latest version of iOS, you can already reply to messages without having to close the app you are using and switch. The most noticeable change in the notification center is the new appearance. Notifications are now easier to read with the white background and black text.

Devices with 3D Touch can interact with the notifications. You can also clear all notifications by pressing the **X** button hard and tap the **Clear All**

**Notifications**. To interact with notifications using 3D touch:

1. Press firmly on a notification.
2. Type, tap or interact with the notification.
3. Once finished, tap the **X** button or simply swipe down.

For non-3D Touch devices, you can attend the notifications by simply swiping to show more options.

A standard text notification looks like a small rectangle on the upper part of the screen. 3D touch allows you to reply to the message without having to open the app anymore.

Other improvements in iOS 10 Notification center:

- Notifications can have description, title as well as subtitle.
- You can set attachments such as images and GIFs.
- You can update the notifications that have been displayed.

# Control Center in iOS 10

Control Center allows you to access some of the basic settings and most important functions. Those settings include:

- Airplane mode
- Wi-Fi
- Bluetooth
- Do not disturb
- Orientation lock
- Brightness
- AirPlayYou can also use AirDrop, flashlight, calculator, timer and camera through control center.

iOS 10 Control center also allows you to access even your HomeKit accessories. This makes it easier for users to modify the device's setting with only few swipes. Another panel also allows you to see the streaming music.

## How to Open Control Center Panels

You can easily access the control center anywhere even from lock screen and while using apps.

1. Tap the bezel from the bottom of the screen.
2. Swipe your finger upwards to show Control Center.

**To switch control center panels:**

3. From the current panel, swipe to the left to access the Now Playing control center panel.
4. Swipe again to the left to enter Home panel.
5. To go back to the first panel, simply swipe to the right.

## How to Disable Control Center on Lock Screen

Control center can be accessed anywhere, even in lock screen. This also allows other people to adjust some of your basic settings without unlocking your device. If you want to disable control center on lock screen, simply follow these steps:

1. Open **Settings** app.
2. Select **Control Center**.
3. Toggle off **Access on Lock Screen**.

## How to Disable Control Center within Apps

There could be times that you accidentally open the control center whenever you need to swipe up from the bottom of the screen. If you need to disable control center within apps, follow these steps:

1. Open **Settings** app.
2. Select **Control Center**.
3. Toggle off **Access Within Apps**.

# Siri in iOS 10

One of the most awesome features of Apple devices is Siri. Tasks are able to be completed faster with the assistance of Siri and there are many things that you can ask such as today's weather, new movies in Netflix, latest songs, nearby restaurants, current stocks and more. You can also ask Siri to enable timer, check mails, play your favorite songs, set reminders and make notes for you. You can also command Siri to make researches.

Siri is now integrated with third-party apps. It has been improved and now smarter than ever. iOS 10 makes Siri your best personal assistant. You can talk to Siri naturally without having to repeat yourself all the time as Siri is now able to comprehend context.

Whether you are doing something, you can command Siri to do other things for you using voice commands.

## How to Activate "Hey Siri" Feature

Siri can be activated without having to touch your device by simply activating the feature "Hey Siri". This works when connected to an active power.

1. Open **Settings app** from Home screen.
2. Select **Siri**.
3. Switch on **Siri**.
4. Switch on "**Hey Siri.**"
5. Simply follow the instructions on screen. It will require you to say "Hey Siri" three times for voice recognition.

When your device is connected to power, simply say "Hey Siri" to open the Siri interface. You can command Siri anything. To dismiss, simply say "**bye**" or "**see you later.**"

# Siri Controls Other Apps

Siri is now able to control third-party apps which can make your experience even more convenient. You can give commands such as order you a car from Uber, look for photos on Pinterest, send your mom a message or send money via Square Cash!

As of now, Siri is integrated with seven apps than can make your experience better than ever! You can use Siri for Messaging, Photo and Video, Workouts, Ride Booking, Payment apps, VoIP calling and CarPlay.

# Siri with CarPlay

You can always command Siri even when you are driving. If you need to make a call, send messages or set a reminder, Siri can help you do those tasks to keep you safe. One of Siri's objectives is to make sure that you keep users eyes on the road and their hands on the wheel.

Activating Siri in CarPlay vary depending on the vehicle used. This is one way to activate Siri, however, it is not recommended.

1. Look for the **Home** button on the screen.
2. Press and hold the Home button.
3. Speak once the waves are displayed on the screen.

The button depends on your location. In UK, the Home button is located on the right side while in the

U.S. the button is on the left side. It appears close to the driver seat. If you want to keep your hands on the wheel, this is another way to activate Siri.

1. Search the voice control button on the wheel.
2. Press and hold the voice control button.
3. Speak once the waves are displayed on the screen.

Activating Siri with CarPlay is easy and you can always complete your tasks even when you are driving. The best way to activate Siri while driving is the voice command "**Hey Siri**". Your device has to be charging while using CarPlay.

Siri also works in the background by providing suggestions based on the information gathered. It can set automatic meetings or reminders depending on the messages exchanged with someone.When typing on the keyboard, suggestions appear based on what you have typed. For instance, you wish to tell a friend the location of the meeting today. Contextual prediction will suggest the address if it is saved in the Calendar app.

# 3

# NEW FEATURES
# IN MESSAGES APP

**M**essages app is the most used app in Apple devices. The latest version of operating system has made huge changes that aim to make the Messages app your ultimate messaging app. It allows you to send stickers, apply personal touch, send attachments like photos and videos and you can also draw short messages.

# Digital Touch

Digital Touch allows you to send hand-drawn sketches, heartbeat, heartbreak, kiss or fireball.

**To send sketches:**
1. Open **Messages** app from Home screen.
2. Tap the **Digital Touch** button. It looks like a heart with two fingers. If you already started typing, the buttons will be hidden and you will have to tap the Show More (>) button to display it.
3. To choose color, tap the **Circle** button on the left side.
4. To show the color palette, tap and hold any of the displayed colors.
5. You can now start to make a sketch on the space provided in the middle.
6. Once you are done, tap the **blue arrow** to send.

## To send a Tap:

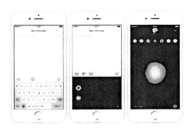

1. Open **Messages** app from Home screen.
2. Tap the **Digital Touch** button. It looks like a heart with two fingers. If you already started typing, the buttons will be hidden and you will have to tap the Show More (>) button to display it.
3. Tao on the canvas.

## To send a Heartbeat:

1. Open **Messages** app from Home screen.
2. Tap the **Digital Touch** button. It looks like a heart with two fingers. If you already started typing, the buttons will be hidden and you will have to tap the Show More (>) button to display it.
3. Using **two fingers** simply tap and hold down on the space provided.

4. Once you release, a heartbeat will be sent automatically.

## To add Digital Touch over a Photo or Video:

1. Open **Messages** app from Home screen.

2. Tap the **Digital Touch** button. It looks like a heart with two fingers. If you already started typing, the buttons will be hidden and you will have to tap the Show More (>) button to display it.

3. Tap the Camera button on the left side under the Circle.

4. To switch the camera from rear to front, tap the camera switch button.

5. To take a photo, tap the **Camera Shutter** at the bottom left. To take a video, tap **the Video Shutter** at the middle. You can record up to ten seconds.

6. Use your finger to make a sketch. You can also add a tap or a heartbeat.

7. Tap the blue arrow to send.

# Handwriting Text Messages

Even though you can already sketch using the Digital Touch feature, you can also use another feature designated for handwriting your messages.

1. Open **Messages** app from Home screen.
2. Rotate your iPhone or iPad to landscape mode to display the handwriting screen.
3. You can choose from **previously sent** handwritten messages or make your own using your finger.
4. Once you are finished, tap **Done**. Additional text can also be added.
5. Tap the up arrow to send your message.

# Bubble Effects in iMessage

iOS 10's new features in iMessage takes your messaging experience to the next level. Once you have installed iOS 10 on your device, you are able to include bubble effects when sending iMessages not only from the Messages app but also from lock screen and notifications. You can include effects in every message that you send like invisible ink, gentle, loud and slam.

## To add bubble effects:

1. Compose a message that you wish to send.

2. **Press firmly** (for devices with 3D touch) or **long press** (non-3D touch) the **Send** button which looks like an up arrow.

3. The Bubble effects will be displayed. Tap the effect that you want to apply on your message.

You can choose from **Slam**, **Loud**, **Gentle** and **Invisible Ink**.

4. Tap **Send** to select the effect that you chose.

## Screen Effects in iMessage

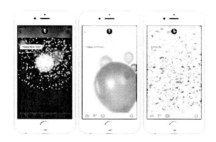

iOS 10 also allows you to send screen effects when sending iMessages not only from Messages app but also from lock screen and notifications. The screen effects that you can choose from are balloons, lasers, confetti, shooting stars and fireworks.

**To add screen effects:**

1. Compose a message that you wish to send.
2. **Press firmly** (for devices with 3D touch) or **long press** (non-3D touch) the **Send** button which looks like an up arrow.
3. Tap the **Screen** tab next to the Bubble tab.

4. Swipe your finger from left to right to try the effects: **balloons**, **confetti**, **fireworks**, **lasers** and **shooting stars**.

5. Tap **Send** button to select the effect that you chose.

## Apps in iMessage

Aside from all the effects and new ways of creating your messages, iOS 10 allows you to install new apps within the Messages app. You can access App Store inside the Messages so you can download apps without having to switch from one app to another. This is also very convenient and time saving. The types if iMessage apps that you can install are payments, food ordering, games, stickers, encrypted messaging, image search and insertion.

## To open apps within iMessage:

1. Open **Messages** app from Home screen.
2. Tap the **Apps** icon which looks like the App Store icon. If you already started typing, the buttons will be hidden and you will have to tap the Show More (>) button to display it.
3. Swipe left and right to switch from one app to another.
4. Tap a sticker or app action to send.

## To see stickers, actions and other apps in full screen:

5. Tap the **Expand** button located from the bottom right.
6. Select any sticker or action that you wish to use.
7. Tap **Send** button.

## To check all apps installed in iMessages:

1. Open **Messages** app from Home screen.
2. Tap the **Apps** icon which looks like the App Store icon. If you already started typing, the buttons will be hidden and you will have to tap the Show More (>) button to display it.

3. Tap the **App Shelf** button located on the bottom left. It looks like four circles.

## To download more apps for iMessage:

1. Open **Messages** app from Home screen.

2. Tap the **Apps** icon which looks like the App Store icon. If you already started typing, the buttons will be hidden and you will have to tap the Show More (>) button to display it.

3. Tap the **App Shelf** button located on the bottom left. It looks like four circles.

4. Tap the **Add** button (+).

# 4

# NEW FEATURES IN PHOTOS APP

Apple redesigned the Photos app in iOS 10 and new features are added that aims to make you remember scenes that you already forgot. It also generates slide shows from your photo memories which you can share to your family and friends.

Photos app has also become smarter as you can quickly search for the photos based on people or location. It uses advanced machine visions which scans your camera roll and determines who is who. Photos app automatically organizes your photos and videos based on place, activity, people and time.

## Memories in Photos

A new tab in the Photos app collects your best pictures or videos into albums based on location, time and people. It also creates a slideshow with music so you can remember the images you have not seen for a long time.

**To find Memories:**

1. Open the **Photos** app from Home screen.
2. Tap **Memories** tab from the bottom of the screen which looks like a play button.
3. Tap a memory to watch.

**To search for memories:**

4. Tap the **Search** button from the upper right corner. It looks like a magnifying glass.

## To play a slideshow:

5. Tap the **memory** you want to watch.

6. Tap the **Play** button.

Slideshows also generate automatic music and theme. You can also change the theme of your slideshows easily. To change the theme:

1. Open the **Photos** app from Home screen.

2. Tap **Memories** tab from the bottom of the screen which looks like a play button.

3. Tap a memory to watch and tap **Play** button.

4. Tap anywhere and tap the **Pause** button from the bottom of the screen.

5. On the menu bar, swipe to check other themes that you can choose such as gentle, uplifting, extreme, dreamy, club and happy.

## To edit title, music, duration, photos and videos in your slideshows:

1. Open the **Photos** app from Home screen.

2. Tap **Memories** tab from the bottom of the screen which looks like a play button.

3. Tap a memory to watch and tap **Play** button.

4. Tap anywhere and tap the **Pause** button from the bottom of the screen.

5. Tap the **Edit** menu from the lower right corner.

6. Tap **photos & videos** or **title, music, duration** to edit your slideshow.

7. Once you are satisfied, tap **Done**.

To save your slide shows, simply tap the **Save Video** button. You can also delete memories by tapping the **Delete Memory** at the bottom of the photo or slideshow.

## Facial Recognition

One of the greatest features of the latest iOS is the facial recognition in the Photos app. A new album

**People** will be included automatically when faces are recognized. This works like the facial recognition in Facebook. It may not be 100 percent perfect but it is very easy to correct.

If you have thousands of pictures in your album, it may take a while for the process to complete. The People album allows you to check catalog of the faces according to how many times they appeared on your photos.

**To view People and Faces:**
1. Open the **Photos** app from Home screen.
2. Tap **Albums**.
3. Select **People** album.
4. Tap the image of the person you want to see to open photos.

Like Memories, an auto slideshow also appears for faces at the top of the screen. You can watch the short video by tapping the **Play** button.

## To add name or rename faces:

1. Tap a **face** that you want to add name or rename.
2. If there is no name yet, tap the + **Add Name**. If there is an incorrect name, tap the **name** to edit it.
3. Simply type the correct name. Suggestions will also be displayed from the Contacts app.
4. Once you are finished, tap **Done**.

## To remove mistakenly recognized faces from the Photos app:

1. Tap a **face** from People album.
2. Tap **Select** button from the upper right corner.
3. If you are not sure of the images you like to correct, simply tap **Show All**. You can also zoom in by tapping **Show Faces**.
4. Pick all the images that you need to select by tapping on them.
5. Tap **Share** button and tap **Not This Person**.

## To add Favorite Faces:

1. In **Photos** App, tap **Albums** and select the **People** album.
2. Tap **Select** from the upper right corner and choose the face that you want to add in your favorites.
3. Tap **Favorite** from the bottom of the screen.
4. Another way is to simply drag the face and place them on top of the screen.

If you want to remove a face from the list of your favorites, simply follow the same steps and tap **Unfavorite** from the bottom of the screen.

## To hide faces from Photos app:

1. Open **Photos** app from Home screen. Tap **Albums** and select the **People** album.
2. Tap **Select** from the upper right corner and choose the face that you want to hide.
3. Tap **Hide** from the bottom of the screen.

Once the faces are hidden, you can see them under the Hidden section. Simply tap Show Less to hide the faces.

**To add new faces:**

1. Open **Photos** app from Home screen. Tap **Albums** and select the **People** album.
2. Tap **Add People** button which is located after all the thumbnails.
3. Choose the people you want to add.
4. Once you are done, tap **Add** button.

You can also merge multiple faces into a single thumbnail by tapping the **Merge** button.

## Markup Editor

iOS 10 is packed with awesome features and one of them is Markup Editor which allows you to make fun photos. You can add doodle, texts and call outs. There is no need to use photo editing apps anymore as the Photos app allows you to add filters, crop and edit your photos.

Even if you can already doodle on your photos and videos within Messages app, you can always have more fun through the Markup Editor within Photos app. This feature only works for photos.

**To open Markup Editor:**
1. Open **Photos** app from Home screen.
2. Choose a photo that you want to edit.
3. Tap the **Edit** icon from the bottom of the screen. This looks like three horizontal lines with circles in each.
4. Tap **More (...)** option then select **Markup**.

**To doodle on your photo:**
5. Tap the **pencil** icon from the bottom of the screen.
6. Choose the color that you want to apply and you can already start doodling.

7. To change the thickness of the pencil, tap the **three horizontal lines** from the right side of the toolbar. You can choose from large, medium and small. Tap to select the thickness that you want to apply.

**To create a Callout:**

8. Tap the **Callout** icon from the bottom of the screen next to the pencil icon.
9. Touch the callout and drag it to the part of the image you want to highlight.
10. To make adjustments of the size, drag the blue dot.
11. To zoom the callout, slide the green dot.
12. If you want to change the callout's color, simply choose the color that you like from the color menu.
13. You can adjust the thickness of the callout by tapping the **three horizontal lines** from the right side of the tool bar.

## To add text:

14. Tap the **Text** icon next to the Callout icon.

15. Tap the text box and select **Edit**.

16. Enter the words you wish to add on your photo.

17. If you want to change the text color, simply choose the color that you like from the menu.

18. If you want to change the font style, simply tap the **double A** from the lower right corner of the screen. Select the **style** that you wish to apply. To change the **font size**, simply move the slider from left to right. You can also change the text alignment if you want it on center, left, right or justified.

19. Once you are finished, simply tap **Done**.

## Moments, Collections and Years

You can check your photos and videos by group which are your moments, collections and years. To move from moments to collections and to years:

1. Open **Photos** app from Home screen.

2. Tap the Back button on the upper left corner to move to Collections or Years. It is labeled like "**<Collections**" or "**<Years**."

3. To go back to a smaller group, simply tap any photo or video.

# 5

# CAMERA AND
# HOME APP

# Camera in iOS 10

The latest operating system of Apple has also made improvements in the Camera app. It is now one of the most powerful tools that for all Apple users. Accessing the Camera app has become easier. In the previous iOS, filters are always still. Now, you can already use filters while making live photos.

## Access Camera from Lock Screen

iOS 10 allows you to access Camera app easier from lock screen. There is no need to search for the Camera icon. All you have to do is to swipe to the left to open the Camera interface. Whenever you need to take a photo of the beautiful scene, you can easily go to Camera app and hit the capture button without missing the event. If you have enabled the Raise to Wake feature, it will be much easier to access Camera as all you have to do is to swipe left and take photos or videos.

## Camera Switch

The camera switch button that allows you to switch from back to front camera has been moved from the top of the screen to the bottom. The filters button has been moved to give space for the camera switch. This makes it easier to take selfies especially on devices with bigger screens.

# Listening While Taking Photos and Videos

Before, launching the Camera app stops the media running in the background such as music. Another improvement in the Camera app is the ability to continue playing your music or podcasts while taking photos or videos.

## Shoot, Edit and Import RAW

With the new version iOS 10, users are now able to experience shooting, editing as well as processing RAW pictures in DNG format using third-party apps.

## Portrait Mode

Users of iPhone 7 Plus can experience the iOS' latest feature which is the Portrait mode. This feature is only exclusive for iPhone 7 Plus. To enable portrait mode:

1. Get the new update **iOS 10.1**.
2. Launch the **Camera** app from Home screen.
3. Swipe your finger on the bottom to move the camera wheel. Look for **Portrait** mode.

4. Tap **Try the Beta** option.

# Home App

The new Home app in iOS 10 allows you to control your HomeKit accessories using your iPhone or iPad. You can easily turn off your appliances or check who is knocking on your door. You can also use your Apple TV to control everything.

Since there are many accessories and with over fifty brands worldwide, Home app allows you to connect all your devices. More accessories are becoming available and compatible with the Home app which allows you to ensure your home security.

## Control Rooms with One Tap

You can easily control the accessories in your rooms with just a tap. With Home app, you can make group accessories according to rooms so you can control them easily depending on where the accessories are located. You can also command Siri to turn the lights off in the garage or turn on the air conditioning unit in your bedroom. Devices with 3D Touch can also perform complicated tasks such as regulating the thermostat or dimming the lights.

## Control Your Home Using Your Voice

Aside from taps, you can also make commands using your voice. For instance, you can make a scene called "Going out" that automatically locks the doors and turns off the lights in all rooms.

## Complete Tasks with Apple TV

Apple TV can also be used to complete tasks even if you are not yet home. You can trigger your home accessories based on your location, time of the day and more. It is very easy to set it up.

## How to Add an Accessory

To use the Home app, you need to make sure that you have **HomeKit-enabled accessories**. Check for the "**Works with Apple HomeKit**" label on the packaging. On your iPhone or iPad, sign in to iCloud using your Apple ID. Turn on iCloud Keychain and Home so you can edit users and accessories.

## Add an accessory:

1. Make sure that the accessory is on and nearby.
2. Launch **Home** app.
3. Tap the **Add Accessory** or the Add (+) button.
4. Your accessory will appear on your screen. Tap the accessory and tap **Allow** when asked to Add Accessory to Network.
5. Scan the HomeKit code on the accessory documentation or on accessory using the camera. You can also enter the code yourself.
6. You can add more details about the accessory such as the room where it is located and its name. This allows Siri to identify your accessories easily.
7. Once you are finished, tap **Done**.

## To edit details of accessory:

1. Launch the **Home** app.

2. Tap the **Home** tab.

3. Select and hold down the accessory that you want to edit.

4. Select **Details**.

   You can add more details to your accessory so that Siri can identify the accessories and their location. You can also assign the type of accessory whether those are lights or switches. Accessories can also be included in Favorites so you can turn them on from Control Center, Apple Watch and Home tab. You can also enable status and notifications to know when the accessories are used.

5. When you are finish editing the details, simply tap **Done**.

If you have many accessories at home, you can easily organize them by creating rooms such as bedroom and living room. This allows you to turn on and off accessories in specific rooms.

## To add room:

1. Launch the **Home** app and select **Rooms** tab.
2. Tap the **list** button (looks like three lines with three dots) in the upper left corner.
3. Tap **Room Settings** then select **Add Room**.
4. Enter the name of the room you want to make, such as Bedroom. You can also change the wall paper for the room by tapping **Take Photo** or **Choose from Existing**.
5. Tap **Save**.

## Assigning accessories to a room:

1. Launch the **Home** app and select **Rooms** tab.
2. Swipe and look for the room where the accessory is located.
3. Tap **Details** and select **Location**.
4. Choose a room for the accessory.
5. Tap **Done**.

# Managing Your Accessories

Once you set up all your accessories, you can easily control them using your iOS device.

- You can turn on and off your accessories from the Rooms tab or from the Home tab.
- You can also use extra features for accessories like thermostats and lights which offer features like temperature controls and brightness.
- You can check the status of your registered accessories with Status and Notifications. For instance, you can check when lights are on.

## Control Multiple Accessories with Scenes

Scenes allow you to manage multiple accessories with only one tap. For instance, you can create a scene named "I'm leaving" which automatically turns off all lights and locks all doors with just a tap.

**To create a scene:**

1. Launch **Homes** app and select **Rooms** tab or **Home** tab.

2. Tap the (+) button then tap **Add Scene**.

3. You can create your own scene or use the suggestions provided.

4. Simply select the accessories you like to add and tap **Done**.

5. To make adjustments in the settings of accessory, simply tap and hold.

6. To see the preview of a scene, tap the **Test This Scene**.

7. Tap **Done** to finish.

You can command Siri to turn on and off your scenes. Of course, you can also add or remove accessories from a scene when necessary.

## Use Siri to Control your Accessories

Once you are done adding accessories to your Home app, you can control them with Siri commands. Here are some commands that you can ask Siri. All commands are based on how you named your accessories and also the scenes.

- Set brightness to 60%.
- I'm back.
- Turn the lights off in my bedroom.
- Set the temperature to 70 degrees.
- Turn the air conditioning unit in the living room.
- Did I lock the main door?

When your iPhone or iPad is locked, Siri cannot control some of the accessories. You will have to unlock your iOS device first before being able to use Siri. For instance, you cannot command Siri to unlock your main door if your device is still locked.

## Delete Data and Reset Accessories

If you need to set up your accessories again in case of moving, you can easily remove home data and reset accessories manually.

## To delete Home data:

1. Open Home app and select Home tab.
2. Tap the arrow pointing to top right .
3. Scroll down and tap **Remove Home**.
4. Tap **Delete** to continue.

# 6

# MUSIC AND MAPS

# Music in iOS 10

Like other Apple built-in apps, Music app also made improvements in the latest version. It is now more simple and easier to navigate.

# New Interface

When you launch the Music app, the first thing that you will see is the **Library** tab. Under the library tab are the music files that you have saved in your device and Apple Music account. The texts are also bigger and the interface is bigger so there is nothing to miss.

The **For You** tab shows the suggested music for you. The **Browse** tab displays the latest songs, playlists and what's going on in the music world. It displays featured events, albums, chart toppers and new music. **Radio** tab allows you to enjoy listening to Beats 1 and other 24/7 worldwide radio stations. **Search** tab allows you to look for music that you preferred and check what other members are listening to.

You can also see all the music that you downloaded from the **Downloaded Music** category under Library. To arrange, remove or add categories under the library, simply tap the **Edit** button from the upper right corner.

Now Playing card looks different now in iOS 10. It has become smaller and you can still navigate around the app while listening to your songs. New buttons are also introduced such as the love and dislike.

## For You

For You tab is now better than ever. Two playlists are added in the For You section (for subscribers): the **My Favorites Mix** and the **My New Music Mix**. Each playlist is updated every week. The suggestions in For You depend on the music that you always listen from the catalog, your love or dislike and your choice of artist and genre.

## Lyrics

You can now check the lyrics of your streaming songs which allow you to sing along.

To open lyrics from a song:

1.  Scroll down to **Up Next** section.
2.  Tap the **three dots** button.
3.  Select **Lyrics**.

This only applies for songs with lyrics included.

*Maps in iOS 10*

Apple has made huge improvements in iOS 10. It is no longer just a simple Maps app that shows you direction. It can do many tasks for you that can make everything more simple and organized. Maps app in iOS 10 is now bigger and smarter. Before, you need to swipe all the time to check the locations. You always had to slide between screens for more details. Now, you can see almost everything in a quick glance.

# New Interface

Maps app has now clearer maps with bright colors and very visible texts. It has a great job for keeping the controls out of the screen until you want them. Both navigational bars from top and bottom are gone and replaced by contextual cards. There is also an overlay for more details, weather and GPS location.

You can also open more details from Maps options. The bottom card displays the search box and suggested locations based on your appointments, daily routine and favorites. This card can be swiped up to display the whole list.

By tapping an address, the contextual card will display the address, driving time and estimate mileage. It may also display photos and websites that you can check. It is also easy to share the location to your friends.

# Book Reservations and Ride

A new tab in Maps is the **Ride** tab. You can select this tab if you need to call a car from **Line**, **Lyft** or **Uber** and more without having to exit the Maps app. When the app has already access, it will display the cars that you can book, estimated cost to destination as well as the time that you have to wait for each. Tap **Book** to go to the next screen where you can request a ride.

Maps app is now integrated with **OpenTable**. You will see **Reservations: OpenTable** button for restaurants that take reservations through OpenTable. Simply tap that button for more options and completing your reservation which only takes two taps. This will be added automatically to your calendar with an alert. If there is a need to cancel your booking, simply go to OpenTable app.

## Intelligent Search and Direction

iOS 10 makes it easier to narrow down the options for **Drinks**, **Shopping**, **Food**, **Travel**, **Services**, **Transport**, **Fun** and **Health**. Tapping the search bar will display those eight options that you can choose from. For instance, if you tap Drinks, it will display Popular, Coffee Shops, Stores, Tea & Juice, Bars, Beer and Wine. Once you tap your chosen category, you can check the list of all suggested places along with the distance, hours, and Yelp price and ratings.

**Directions** also have better interface than before. The **bold details** and brighter screen is excellent for quick look information. Large buttons and Siri can also help you out when you are driving so your eyes can stay on the road.

Enabling **turn-by-turn** allows you to search for local gas, fast food and coffee. You can also give command to Siri to search for nearby gas stations or coffee place and Maps app will automatically show you options and make a stop according to your answer.

## Parked Car

Another added feature in iOS 10 is the Parked Car marker. Your device can recognize where it last interacted with your car and make a mark in the Maps app. This works if your car has CarPlay or Bluetooth. It also displays the distance and time to reach the parking area. If your Maps Destination is included in your Today view, it can also show you where you parked your car.

# 7

# NEWS, CLOCKS AND VOICEMAIL TRANSCRIPTIONS

# News App in iOS 10

Like the Music app, News app is also redesigned creatively. It has now a brand new icon and provides you more customized **For You** tab which has clear sections. You can now easily see the news that you are most concerned with.

## New Interface

The interface of the News app has been entirely changed. Some details are already in bold such as the date and you can see your current location as well as the weather above the screen. Headlines are also bigger and you can easily notice the top and trending articles.

With iOS 10, there is no need to scroll down all the time to see the articles as the content is divided into many sections. You can see at least six stories per section with big images. By tapping the arrow on the right side, you can check more content of each section in a new page. The new page has subsections: Latest News or Today's Best.

## For You

The iOS 10 makes the For You section more personalized. There is date and weather included at the top which gives a newspaper touch. The headlines are in bold with video attachments that you can watch. For You can also personalize this section based on the topics that you subscribed to. The more you use it, the more it becomes intelligent. You can easily see the stories that are very important to you.

## News Notifications

Another change in iOS 10 is the option for notifications. When you first open the app, you will have an option to enable the notifications from publishers that you follow such as CNN, Bloomberg and Washington Post. If you had it disabled, you can turn them on manually.

To enable notifications:

1. Go to **Favorites**.
2. Tap the **bell** icon from the upper left corner.
3. Tap the switch to turn on the notifications for each channel.

The iOS 10 News allows you to sign in to your paid subscriptions so you can read all the articles without any limit. There is also an option to sign up for new subscriptions or download the app of the publishers.

# Clock App in iOS 10

The Clock app is also updated with its brand new **Bedtime** tab. This feature is designed to help you sleep and wake up on the right time. There is a reminder that alerts you when you should go to sleep and alarm to wake you up.

**To activate Bedtime:**

1. Open the **Clock** app from Home screen.
2. Tap the **Bedtime** tab from bottom of the screen.
3. Tap **Get Started**.

4. It will ask you to choose your desired time to wake-up. Once you set the time, tap **Next**.

5. Select the days of the week you want the alarm go off then tap **Next**.

6. Select how many hours of sleep you need each night then tap **Next**.

7. Decide when you would like a bedtime reminder. Tap **Next**.

8. Choose the sound you want to hear when you wake up then tap **Next**.

9. Tap **Save** to finish.

## To change Bedtime settings:

1. Open the **Clock** app from Home screen.

2. Tap the **Bedtime** tab from the bottom of the screen.

3. Tap the **Options** button from the upper left corner to change the settings for bed time reminder, days of the week, alarm sound and volume.

4. On Bedtime dial, touch and drag the **moon** icon to adjust your bedtime. Touch and drag the **bell** icon to adjust your wake up time.

5. To enable or disable the Bedtime feature, simply tap the switch next to Bedtime.

# Voicemail Transcriptions in iOS 10

Visual Voicemail is gradually becoming one of the features in major carriers. Apple has added voice mail transcriptions feature in iOS 10 and it is very easy to use. This feature is available for iPhone 7 Plus, iPhone 7, iPhone SE, iPhone 6s Plus and iPhone 6s.

## To use voicemail transcriptions in iOS 10:

Before you start, it is best to check if your carrier supports Visual Voicemail. If yes, it will be automatically available in your Phone app.

1. Open the **Phone** app.
2. Tap **Voicemail** tab from the bottom of the screen.
3. Tap a voicemail message you want to read.
4. A text above the play button will appear and that is the transcription.
5. If you want to listen to the voicemail, simply tap the **Play** button. You can also raise your device to listen if **Raise to Listen** feature is enabled.

**To share voicemail transcriptions to others:**

If the transcription can be useful to your family or friends, you can share the message easily. You can also select parts of the transcript.

1. Open the **Phone** app.
2. Tap **Voicemail** tab from the bottom of the screen.
3. Tap the voicemail message you want to share.
4. Touch and hold the transcript until more options appear.
5. To select parts of the transcript that you want to share, drag the highlight or selection bars.

6. Tap Share option.

7. Choose the app you want to use for sharing the transcript.

## To add Calendar event using voicemail transcript:

If the voicemail transcript has important information such as time and date (words that are underlined) you can easily add this information to your Calendar directly from the voicemail.

1. Open the **Phone** app.

2. Tap **Voicemail** tab from the bottom of the screen.

3. Tap the voicemail message that contains the information.

4. Tap the underlined words such as date or time to view more options.

5. Tap **Create Event**.

6. Enter more information about the event.

7. To finish, tap **Add**. This will automatically save the event in your Calendar app.

## To report your feedback:

Even though voicemail transcriptions work, some transcriptions are not transcribed well. You can always report your experience to Apple by giving your feedback.

1. Open the **Phone** app.
2. Tap **Voicemail** tab from the bottom of the screen.
3. Tap a voice message that is not transcribed well.
4. Choose between **Useful** or **Not useful** from the bottom of the text.

## To fix not working transcriptions:

If you experience some problems with voicemail transcriptions, learn what to do:

- Make sure that your Carrier supports Visual Voicemail feature.
- Check if your Carrier has made an update.
- Check for new iOS updates.
- Reboot your device.

- Make sure that cellular network is enabled and working.
- Reset your network settings.

# 8

# BASIC TROUBLE SHOOTING TIPS

H ere are the most common iOS 10 issues and their quick solutions.

## Device Stopped Working Completely

If your device suddenly stopped working:

1. Plug in your device into PC or Mac.
2. Launch iTunes.
3. Perform Recovery Mode by press and holding the On/Off and Home button until Recovery Mode screen appears.

4. Select Update when iTunes asked if you want update or restore.

# Battery Life Problem

There are many ways to reduce the consumption of your battery life.

- You can reduce your device's **Brightness** setting from Control Center. Simply swipe up from the bottom of the screen and adjust screen brightness.
- Another way to resolve battery life problem is to adjust the **Auto-Lock** time to seconds. To make adjustments, open Settings app, select Display & Brightness and tap Auto-Lock.
- Turning off **Raise to Wake** can also help in preserving the battery. This feature turns on your device whenever you pick it up and if you need to save battery, it is best to disable this feature.
- Enable **Low Power Mode**. This feature stops refreshing all apps running in the background

and can increase the battery life. This feature prompts once your battery hits 20 percent. Even if you still have over 20 percent, you can always enable this feature by going to **Settings**, tap **Battery** and toggle on **Low Power Mode**.

- Disable **Background App Refresh** feature. This feature is one of the main consumers of battery. Open **Settings** app, tap **General** and select **Background App Refresh**. Toggle off all apps that you do not want to refresh automatically.
- Turn off **Wi-Fi** when not needed.

## Wi-Fi and Bluetooth Problems

If you are experiencing problems with Wi-Fi connectivity or Bluetooth, here is the fix:

1. Open **Settings** app from Home screen.
2. Select **General**.
3. Tap **Reset**.
4. Tap **Reset Network Settings**.

Performing Reset Network Settings keeps all your data except wireless connections. You will have to enter Wi-Fi passwords again.

## How to Disable Press Home to Unlock

The old way Swipe to Unlock is now replaced by Press Home to Unlock. There is no way to bring it back but for devices with Touch ID sensors, it is possible to disable Press Home to Unlock by activating Rest Finger to Open. This feature allows you to simply rest your finger to unlock your device.

1. Open **Settings** app from Home screen.
2. Select **General**.
3. Tap **Accessibility**.
4. Tap **Home button** and toggle on **Rest Finger to Open**.

## How to Adjust Home Button Haptic Feedback

For iPhone 7 users, the Home button haptic feedbacks can be too strong or too weak. You can always adjust the feedback according to your preferences.

1. Open **Settings** app from Home screen.
2. Select **General**.
3. Tap **Home** button.
4. There are three options that you can choose from. Try each and select your preferred strength.
5. To finish, tap **Done**.

## How to Solve Issue with Touch ID

If Touch ID suddenly stopped working, learn what to do:

1. Open **Settings** app from Home screen.
2. Select **Touch ID & Passcode**.
3. Enter your passcode. Toggle **off** Apple Pay and iTunes & App Store.
4. Restart your device.
5. Open Settings app again.
6. Select Touch ID & Passcode.

7. Enter your passcode. Toggle **on** Apple Pay and iTunes & Appstore.
8. Enter your password when asked.

If this solution did not fix the problem, you may need to delete your fingerprint and add them back.

1. Open **Settings** app from Home screen.
2. Select **Touch ID & Passcode**.
3. Enter your passcode.
4. Tap **Delete Fingerprint**.

After deleting your fingerprint, simply register it again.

## Maps Transit Widget Not Working

Maps Transit Widget provides schedules for subway and bus routes. If the widget stopped working, learn what to do:

1. Open **Settings** app.
2. Select **General**.
3. Tap **Accessibility**.
4. Tap **Speech**.

5. Enable **Speak Screen**. This solution will force the widget to work.

## iMessage Effects Not Working

If iMessage effects do not appear, here is what to do:

1. Open **Settings** app.
2. Select **Messages**.
3. Disable **iMessage** and enable it again.

If turning on and off the iMessage did not work, you may need to turn off Reduce Motion.

1. Open **Settings** app.
2. Select **General**.
3. Tap **Accessibility**.
4. Tap **Reduce Motion** and toggle it off.

## Siri Stopped Working

If you experience problems with "Hey Siri" feature after updating to iOS 10, here's are the solutions that you can try.

- Open Settings app and check if the "Hey Siri" feature is enabled.

- Disable "Hey Siri" feature and turn off Siri. Restart your device and enable again Siri and Hey Siri.

- Reset All Settings. Go to **Settings** app, select **General**, tap **Reset** and select **Reset All Settings**.

## Duplicated Music Files and Playlists

Many users have experienced this problem after getting the latest operating system. Here are some solutions to fix:

- Connect your device to PC or Mac and open iTunes. Sync your device.

- Delete all music files and sync again with iTunes.

- Delete each song or playlist one by one.

# CONCLUSION

In Conclusion, I would like to thank you for purchasing this guide. I am sure that this guide will cover all the basic needs to master and use the latest iOS version until it lasts. Good Luck!

• • • • • • • •

# REFERENCES

- http://www.apple.com/ios/home/

- http://www.imore.com/ios-10

- http://www.iphonelife.com/content/how-to-use-voicemail-transcription-ios-10

- http://www.digitaltrends.com/mobile/ios-10-problems/

CPSIA information can be obtained
at www.ICGtesting.com
Printed in the USA
FSOW02n0809201216
28749FS

9 781540 671974